ANKUR HORA

Worldwide Publishing by
Pendown Press
Powered by

PENDOWN PRESS
Powered by **Gullybaba Publishing House Pvt. Ltd.,**
An ISO 9001 & ISO 14001 Certified Co.,
Regd. Office: 2525/193, 1st Floor, Onkar Nagar-A, Tri Nagar, Delhi-110035
Ph.: 09350849407, 09312235086
E-mail: info@pendownpress.com
Branch Office: 1A/2A, 20, Hari Sadan, Ansari Road, Daryaganj, New Delhi-110002
Ph.: 011-45794768
Website: PendownPress.com

First Edition: 2020
Price: ₹259/-
ISBN: 978-93-89601-92-3

All Rights Reserved

All the ideas and thoughts in this book are given by the author and he is responsible for the treatise, facts and dialogues used in this book. He is also responsible for the used pictures and the permission to use them in this book. Copyright of this book is reserved with the author. The publisher does not have any responsibility for the above-mentioned matters. No part of this publication may be reproduced, distributed, or transmitted in any form or by any means, including photocopying, recording, or other electronic or mechanical methods, without the prior written permission of the publisher and author.

Layout and Cover Designed by Pendown Graphics Team
Printed and Bound in India by Thomson Press India Ltd.

Contents

About Me

CHAPTER 1

Clarity = Power   1

CHAPTER 2

Everything Lies in "WHY"   7

CHAPTER 3

"Qualified Leads=Lifeline of your Business"   13

CHAPTER 4

Get Instant Lead Framework   17

CHAPTER **5**

World Class Marketer   21

CHAPTER **6**

The Only Choice   27

CHAPTER **7**

Activate Lead Engine   33

About Me

World's Leading Authority In Nano Video Creation!!

During My College day, was an Extreme Introvert Guy... But...Whenever I used to See a Success story...I used to get Instigated with one message in Head. I would Also Touch Millions of Lives One Day...Finally, Today, I have developed an eye of a Great Marketeer, Copywriter & a Story-Shower. I am a Spiritual geek turned Freedompreneur, a Pranic Healer......A Yoga practitioner, married to a super Healer and father of 2.....On a Mission to serve 100,000 Freedompreneurs living freedom driven lifestyle Using Nano Videos. I successfully run 2 SAP Driven Manufacturing ventures with a team strength of 250 people.

My 19 Years Journey of self-exploration and business improvement, Really helped me to Evolve. I've been trained by Best trainers like T Harv Eker, Blair Singer, Mac Attram, Zolton, Larry Gillman & Many More World Class Coaches.

CHAPTER 1

Clarity = Power

Are you struggling to increase your revenues?

Are you struggling with a lack of customers in your business?

Are you finding ways to scale-up your marketing, but you are stuck with your digital marketing company/agency?

Are you dependent on the inflow of Leads from your Sales field staff and still the lead and customer bank is Dry?

If you can resonate with these Painful Facts, no one better than me can feel it. I am sure as an Entrepreneur, if you have this pain at whatever stage your business is, this is something, which needs immediate addressing. When I say Immediate addressing, then it means that you need to get awareness first that this is happening in my business for ___Months/Years.

Would you love to know, how I coped with when I was struggling with the same, by just asking myself a few questions?

1. Are you in awareness….that you are struggling….with the challenge of Lack of Leads and customers finally?

   Answer: _____

   _____

2. How much loss did you incur in your business in last _____ Months/years?

   Answer: _____

   _____

3. What has it cost you? Or What are you experiencing in the different spheres of your life?

   Answer: _____

   _____

Mental Sphere: _____

Emotional Sphere: _____

Spiritual Sphere: _____

For E.g. I enjoy the freedom and that's my core value. When my business was struggling with scarcity of leads, then at that time, I used to feel very drained. I would feel that I need to work hard and meet customers and generate more business for my company. In fact, I always had a burning desire to serve people, but since my own business became my enemy, I kept on compromising on my mission to serve people.

Therefore, I would recommend you to write in all spheres of your life….Trust me, this would give you great clarity by the end of this exercise.

Clarity = Power

P.S: Would you agree that 100% honesty towards your own self is required to perform this exercise?

Yes, it would work and give maximum clarity, if you promise with me. Now, to be honest with yourself while doing all exercises given in the Book,....I can visualize your success...and that really makes me super-excited right now.

4. For how much more time, do you wish to continue in this same vicious circle?

Answer: _____

_____

5. Are you sure and committed to read the book till the end and take the necessary actions?

Answer: _____

_____

Remember: Either you can trust or you cannot. Either a female is pregnant or she is not, she can never be partially pregnant. Either I am honest or dishonest, I can never be partially honest.

In this way, you gotta trust yourself and me 100%, Now..... Go ahead with super-strong conviction. If you do this, the same formulae will give you faster results... Do you want that?

Great, I congratulate you for your honesty and sincere work. Lemme tell you, it takes courage to face reality. Remember, when you participated last in the game of running, you didn't go to the finish line, but, you went through the finish line.....I'm certain for your success, the way you are performing...

If you've not filled the above questions, better flip the page back and ask yourself one question.

"How this brain pattern of seeing things and not completing them is costing me in my life?"

Go Ahead, Yes, you did it and you made me feel proud of the being you are and the efforts you are ready to take and come out of your comfort zone.

"Getting in Awareness + Being honest to yourself + Confrontation= Clarity"

Lemme make this simpler for U:

"Awareness+ Honesty+ Confrontation=Clarity"

Now, since you have got clarity and have confronted it, lemme share, what's in it for you, which you will get by the end of this book:

1. You will become an authority in your industry and your face would be synonymous with the product industry you are in.

   Are you thinking it's a big commitment to make? I want you to play big with greater power now. Are you ready for what's next gonna be?

2. You will never ever face the scarcity of leads and your lead bank would be abundant and would have more than what you have ever desired...Would that yield you better returns in your business and deliver contentment in every sphere of your life?

3. You would never have to be dependent completely either on your digital marketing agency, or just the field sales staff. In fact, you would get the power to empower your customer and finally you would get a choice to choose your customer, rather than customer choosing you. Do you want that in your business?

CHAPTER 2

Everything Lies in "WHY"

T Harv Eker says, "If your **WHY** gets clear, your how becomes **easy**."

Thus, let's get to the core and understand why this state has come into your life? Why does your business need more leads and customers than it has now? Let's understand the different sources and dive straight in what could be the choices which have got us to this state:

Lemme Ask you A few questions: **"Put a hand on your heart and say, "I'm in complete awareness and I am ready for a confrontation which will give me ultimate clarity."**

1. Is your Business dependent on the word-of-mouth and referrals and is it giving you enough leads which your business needs?

   Answer: _____

   _____

2. Is your business dependent on the existing customers as the only source and is it fulfilling the amount of revenue as expected?

Answer: _____

_____

3. Are you in awareness with what the right number (We call it... **Nano Number**) is of leads that your business needs and what's the cost you pay when your business doesn't get that number of leads?

Answer: _____

_____

4. Does your Business have any budget or strategy in place for the creation of a lead engine?

Answer: _____

_____

5. Has there been some past experience in the context of marketing or sales, which is holding you back for taking aggressive actions further?

Answer: _____

_____

6. Is there any confusion regarding the selection of the right medium/platform for marketing and the right methodology for doing the same?

Answer: _____

_____

7. Is your business getting the right segment of customers whom it should cater to or is your campaign running targeting the right customer segment?

Answer: _____

_____

8. Is the target customer selected to whom we are marketing, giving us rich profits or are we happy with negligible margins thinking "Market is too competitive?"

Answer: _____

_____

9. Do you have a sales team who is not performing up to the expectations?

Answer: _____

_____

10. Have you expected that your sales team would search the leads themselves or are they constantly provided with the leads to make the process shorter and easier?

Answer: _____

_____

Hey, raise your right hand and pat your back for the **"Courage and Honesty"** you showed while confronting these hard facts. Trust me! This will allow you to stay in awareness and give you clarity in the end. Lemme say from my soul: **"I am sure for your victory and I congratulate you for completing the**

first, but the most challenging step". Lemme share 2 Quotes which you would love certainly;

> "Clarity and Freedom go hand in hand".

AND

> "Clarity after confrontation will give you Authority".

After confronting the challenges, in the above questionnaire, the first step for which you got to get aware is that "U need to get more freedom by spending your most valuable resources (i.e.) Time is the most important domain of your business (i.e.) Marketing.

I can understand your situation, as, I used to give 80 per cent time in operations/process Building and with the leftover time, I used to focus on Sales and Marketing. However, I realised a great shift in my being when I read.

> " Marketing eliminates or reduces the need for sales ."

Thus, first, you need to promise yourself that your at least 40 % of time should get invested in marketing. When I say marketing, it does not mean sales calls or meetings. It's about building a lead engine by doing the right marketing. Thus, once you get the freedom from the operations or service, or production side of your business, then certainly it will give you more clarity, further resulting in more Authority. Lemme make it more memorable by making it simpler for you and

I've tailored a theory for you, V2V Theory of Marketing...

Vicious to Virtuous Shift is all That u Need at this Moment. Don't know the process of the shift?... Hold... If you think first, I will have resources like people and processes for doing the right marketing to resolve this challenge, then lemme share something. This is also a mind-freak which your mind is playing right now. So, you have to rewire your brain and mind. You gotta get the awareness that I need to step in a virtuous circle from the vicious circle thinking 2 facts.

"I will fire, then I will aim rather than I will aim & then I will fire"

AND

"Once I start getting going, I will get good at it"

Bonus: If your brain is saying now to yourself, that I'm not a marketer and I haven't done it in past, then you need to ask yourself a simple question.

"Which thing/activity in my life did I learn without repetition?"

Yes, from walking to eating, to studying or reading or doing any activity in life, you have learned with practice..

Or

"If your mind is saying to you "How would it be perfect?"

Then also, please command to your mind that "Perfection is an illusion"

"First Resource and Then start"

Moral: Don't get in the trap of chicken or egg first, rather, just step out and don't allow your mind to play mind-freaks and dive straight in a virtuous circle instead of staying in a vicious circle forever.

CHAPTER 3

"Right Qualified Leads= Lifeline of your Business."

Congratulations for Being a warrior till here and confronting every fact now with grace... I truly appreciate the same... So, by now:

Would you agree that lead is a lifeline for your business?

Do you realise that leads are directly related to your revenues and profits in your business?

Great, this acceptance with grace will allow you to enter a zone of freedom once you get the right marketing in place which will activate your lead engine.

So, first code in your brain that

"Leads=Freedom"

Yes, you need to stay in this awareness that your business needs a lead engine which will:

Leads--Prospect--Customer--Money--Freedom

Do you wanna have access to a zone where you choose your customer?

Lemme share a small story of my own company of manufacturing wood polymer composites, named ecoste (www.ecoste.in).

I started that in 2013. Initially, I was myself doing the sales and marketing and I had no idea of what's the difference between both these terms. Thereafter, I started appointing a sales team with great hope, but, they were unable to generate the results, even the break even level. I thought I appointed the wrong people, so I got the new team this time.

In 2015, I got the team of 25 People with 3 layer hierarchy and till 2017, this team working in Pan India doubled the turnover. However, the bad debts and late payments worsened the whole plan to the extent that I had to fire the whole team overnight.

I remember one night, I was feeling broken to the extent that I started crying, placing my head on my wife's shoulder. I was feeling utterly helpless for the first time to the greatest extent. I had then only 2 choices to make:

1. Go to my dad and say I must close down this business since it has ceased to work as I'm not able to align sales

2. Find an alternate strategy and go to the core of why it is not happening the way I am expecting...

Friends, The Divine made me choose the 2nd path that night and gave me the strength to find that invisible root & why for my failures.

What I got as an answer after a few days of inner reflection was just one liner:

"There is **no right marketing** in place which would create **a lead engine** in my business"

This statement made a dent in my mind and I took it as a challenge. I resolved to be the world's greatest marketer and started my journey. The days initially were of lot of hits and trials and a lot of failures too, however, my passion for being a marketer kept me ignited.

At that time, I used to get 10 leads a day which wasn't sufficient to feed huge manufacturing and that too with no field team in place. Thus, I initiated some right marketing actions which I will share with you soon, which created massive awareness and increased the lead flow to 40 a day...This flow of leads started giving us a choice to choose our customer in a year's time to decide whether we should continue working with that customer or not. It gave us the freedom of not to go to any client and they came to our office and worked on our own terms of 100% Advance.

Are you thinking that I am also facing similar challenges, but will this methodology work in my business or not?

"Trust the Process"
and
"Keep the faith"

It's tried and tested on different types and scales of business and it works in a pervasive way...

So, once you get the lead engine built and it starts, you will experience that you will have the power of creating an Inside sales machine and you don't need to depend on the massive outside force... For this also, I will share my strategies on how after initiating the lead engine, I created an inside sales machine. Now we have only 2 Senior sales professionals on-field and a team of 8 Inside sales experts. They don't go anywhere and our engine generates 100 leads a day and now in the next FY, we have the plan to take this number to 200 to generate 2 X revenue in 20-21.

But, at the core is not inside sales machine. It is first the lead engine which was created by doing the right methodology which I will share in the next chapter and thereafter you would also need an inside sales machine to handle and generate revenue and profits at your own terms. This has given me a great feeling of security, freedom, choice and growth. I am certain in your case by seeing your courage. I now pray for your multifold success.

CHAPTER 4

Get Instant Lead Framework

Do u wanna Framework to Get Instant leads?

Once you've realised the power of a lead engine in your business, now the time has come to uncover the formulae. This formula has given me millions and has the power to make me and you a billionaire. More than Money, the freedom it'll give you, that's something which even money can't buy for U. So, I'm sharing with you the formulae which have been developed after....so many trials, errors, failures, feedbacks, and I have invested a great amount of my time in developing this. So, the GIL (Get Instant Leads) Formula is:

> **Get Instant Leads= (Targeted Traffic* Conversion Mastery)$^{Nano\ Videos}$**

Thus, GIL (Get Instant Leads) Framework is not about the difficult digital marketing, but it's about making the concept of core marketing which will make all your efforts go in the right direction, from now, producing the right results for you ever in your business.

Let's make it so simple. There releases an English action movie and its trailer video comes on Youtube sponsored by Book my show. Now, you love the English action movies and after seeing the full trailer video, you go to book my show and book movie tickets.

Thus, if you evaluate this whole situation, is there a message shown to the right audience in the right method? The Method is using a powerful "**Video**". Lastly, the message in the video hooked you certainly to take action.

Just this much...yes... Lemme ask you 2 simple questions:

1. Do you just want to know and remember this GIL Framework?

OR

2. Do you wanna practice and master the formula and get massive results?

Thus, if you feel your answer is yes for first question, you must take 3 deep breaths and ask another question to yourself:

What is costing me to survive in my business without having a strong lead engine?

After that, take a deep breath, and resume reading...

If your answer is yes for question 2 only, then for sure you have a calling from your being to be a great marketer. However, if you need to understand and go in depth to understand the GIL Framework, there is no escape route for one thing...Are you excited to hear that one thing...? Hmm...U Guys are Hungry... Flip to the next page...

CHAPTER 5

World Class Marketer

Yes, you read right...!!!

Do you want to be a world-class marketer?

This is why I want to initiate an installation which is already in each one of you Now. So, put a hand on your heart and say, **"I am a world-class marketer"**.

Great, Applaud for the efforts made till now...Keep up the pace...The Secret key to unlock the Get Instant Leads is that you need this **installation** at your being level, and need to feel that you are a great marketer.

In this chapter, I will unfold several hacks & formulas which once used will keep the things very simple for you. And I here present to you a 4 Square principle to give an immense clarity on the GIL formulae. The **4 Square Principle** represents:

1. Market

2. Message
3. Medium
4. Method

So, it's time to dive straight in **4M** and let's chop them off one by one. The first M being **Market**, you have to target and work with the right market. The niche needs to be clear. Everything starts from this & it's the core of the same. Thus, we @ecoste were making videos for everyone, however, since last one year we are focused on working only with government organisations. Now, we are a CPWD-approved brand. We are now making the videos only targeting government architects, engineers and contractors.

Thus, my mentor says, **"When you work with everybody, you work with nobody."** Thus, now we are just focused on **one target group** which is giving us **4X results** by just doing the same efforts but for the focused right market, we want to work with.

I hope that getting to the selection of the right niche and target market is the most important exercise when it comes to getting to the core of the marketing. Thus, now let's get to the core of the 2nd M (*i.e.*) **Message.** When it comes to message, the most important point to get to core is to understand 3 Things (**NDP Analysis for Message**):

1. What are the **needs** of your target market?
2. What are the **desires** of your target market?
3. What are the **Problems** of your target market?

Thus, the most important mistake the majority of the companies do is that even when they target the right customer, they deliver a message to them which doesn't resonate or synchronise with the target market. The only reason is that when you start the marketing without understanding the NDP of your target market, it will be only a game of fluke. Thus, its relevance is massive and this step can't be ignored.

Would you agree that this exercise of the NDP would get Laser clarity in your Message? Let's make things more clear. Puma interviewed about the Gym wear clothing,

"What's the **biggest need, desire and problem** for them?"

They understood after asking lots of customers and they found that

1. Need: To get something that absorbs sweat and odour. To look smart when they wear them in the gym & at home. Lastly, to make them look slimmer and super fit and give an image of a fitness freak.

2. **Desire:** To give away a free pair of gloves in some fabric which would give a better grip. Secondly, some said that they would need a perfume which is designed to spray on that dry fit material customised to absorb instant sweat...
3. **Problems:** The clothes they wear, do not absorb the sweat, gives them odour and it depletes their energy to work out more intensely.

Thus, the NDP can be resolved by **WIIFM... (What in it for Me)**

Thus, now instead of designing the message as "Dry-Fit', they decided "Keeps You Dry."

After you have done with the NDP analysis, the message has to undergo a **Marketable Consumable Methodology (MCM).**

Lastly, every message has to be backed up with Action. Thus, lemme make it simpler for you by saying **MTA (Message to Action) Principle.**

Thus, in every message there can be multiple actions or even solid action which you've heard as **CTA (Call To Action).** The CTA button is something you must have seen many times, for eg: Get free copy now, Buy now, Get access now and can be customised like ways...

Right Message:

NDP* MCM* MTA

Thus, if you follow this formulae, which has a complete science in 3 theories and you agglomerate them, it will get you to the right message for sure. Moreover, as said prior, everything you and I have learned with practice. Similarly, your 4th message which you will design for the video, email or any marketing communication will be better than your 1st one...So, Just GO for it...

Hope things are super easy and clear so far!!

Great, appreciate your interest so far and let's now calibrate with the **next M (*i.e.*) Medium.** This M is very important and this is where I would love to share my mistakes and findings.

Lemme ask you, it must have happened with the majority that we get stuck when it comes to marketing—what platform should we use Fb or Instagram or LinkedIn or Youtube or Email etc..However, what I learned from my mistake was that I was too much stuck for many years and used to hop between one platform to another. Do you wanna know Why?

The only reason was, I wasn't clear which my market was and what message would work for them. Thus, after I got clarity of my market and message, I became so much focused on what medium they would prefer to see my message. Therefore, selection of medium is very important, but it has to go in the right sequence. Thus, for example, someone who wants to market his or her product/service but it's B2B, and if he or she does that on InstaGram, it would not work. Thus, the selection criteria have to inculcate that your message has to target your right audience at the right platform.

So, getting overwhelmed and more valued than expected? That's what I want for each one of you. Your every customer should get a massive 10X value for the money you are exchanging with them. Thus, at this juncture, I would introduce you to the **last M (*i.e.*) Method.**

The Method is same which says what methodology you want to use or rather I should say, what method does your market want to consume your message. This is something which is very important as even if you do all 3 M's in the right way, but make a mistake in choosing the wrong method, the method is something which now allows me to introduce you with **one single medium** from which I got the maximum success.

Do you want the access to that medium which allows our brand Ecoste to get 100 leads a day without spending a single penny on paid advertisement? Yes, you read it right and that too by just **investing 15 Min a day**… My friend!

Trust me, this one thing holds a value in my life and business worth millions. But, I am on a mission to empower you by activating your lead engine in your business using the power of that one method….Flip to Next Page to Get An Access NOW…

CHAPTER 6

The Only Choice

Yes...The only choice!!... I mean that in today's busy time where the attention time has reduced to less than 3 seconds, there is something we need to understand, i.e. the pulse of today's audience.

Thus, the only choice which has given me now and will always give in future as well is the **Nano Videos**...Yes, **Nano Video's**

You are thinking videos... For what medium or message or market?

I can understand that you are overwhelmed.... with the in-depth understanding and now you are curious and excited... about how videos will help U in getting your message (to your right audience).

Just take a deep breath and let's go step by step from here. Moreover, till now we were laying down the foundation through the required information. However, now the time has come to get you out of your comfort zone and get in real action...Are you ready... or little scared…? Don't worry, I'm here for every help and say to your inner voice now... **I am a world-class marketer…**

So, allow me to share some important insights about the video marketing.

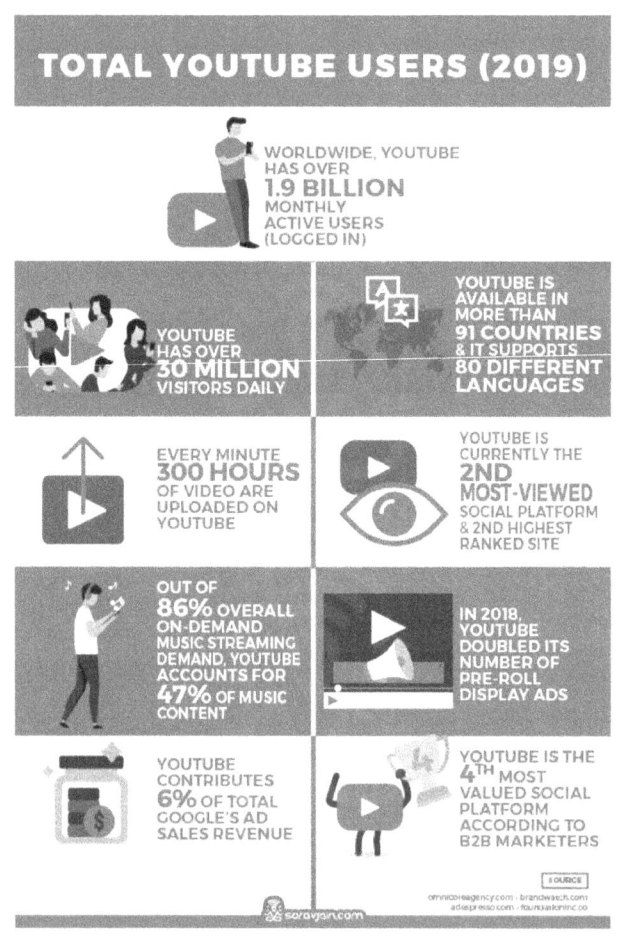

The Only Choice

VIDEO MARKETING FACTS

92% of mobile video viewers share videos with others. —Invodo

65% of executives have visited a vendor's site after watching a video. —Forbes

70% of marketing professionals report that video converts better than any other medium. —MarketingProfs

The average internet user spends **88%** more time on a website with video. —Mist Media

1.8 Million Words is the VALUE of one minute of VIDEO. —Dr. James McQuivey, Forrester

Get Instant Leads

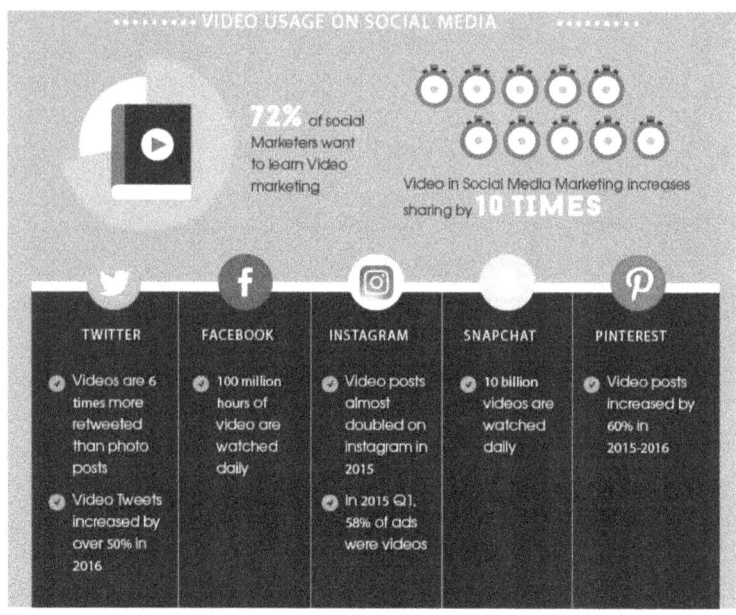

The Massive YouTube Ecosystem

The Only Choice

FAST FACTS

88% of video marketers have reported being satisfied with the ROI of their videos' success on social media.

VIDEO MARKETERS ALSO SEE
66% MORE QUALIFIED LEADS IN A YEAR AND OVER 50% INCREASE IN BRAND AWARENESS.

Users spend 88% more time on a website *with videos* as compared to those without.

54% of online consumers report they actually want *even more video content.*

73% of consumers claim videos have influenced them when making purchasing decisions.

87% OF MARKETERS **USE VIDEO** AS PART OF THEIR DIGITAL MARKETING STRATEGIES IN THE LAST YEAR ALONE.

93%
SOCIAL MEDIA VIDEO MARKETING

Audiences are *95% more likely* to remember a brand's *call to action* after a video.

Thus, when it comes to method, the only method which works today, and will in fact more aggressively in the near future, is Nano videos. I know you must be thinking **100's of questions** like:

- I am shy about making videos
- I have not made videos prior
- I have not learned the art of creating videos
- I do not know how to shoot and edit professionally
- Would it really work for me?
- Would it work for my business?

Think about it. **People remember...**

20% **30%** **70%**

20% of what they hear   30% of what they see   An amazing 70% of what they see & hear!

- I don't have that much budget for the same?
- I don't have content for the same
- I don't know how to structure the content of videos
- On what topics should I create videos?
- Will my audience watch these videos?
- On which platform will my audience watch these videos?
- Why should I do it?
- No one in my industry is doing the same
- Am I smart enough or would I look good to my audience?
- Is my communication worth acceptance from the audience?

Thus, all these questions are pretty valid and acknowledge your concern..Trust me, at some stage of my life, even I had some or the other question popping in my mind. However, I wanna make it simpler for you by telling you the truth of the hour by narrating my own story...Friends, Exactly, the same mind freaks/objections, I also had, but, I just came out of it using **one technique** which I will be sharing with you in my one day workshop of Get Instant Leads. Are you thinking, why am I not sharing that now?

Lemme share, **"Some things can only be experienced"**. Thus, you have to experience that and I assure you that you will get an answer to all of them on that **one full power-packed single day** itself. Log on to www.ankurhora.com NOW and enroll yourself for the upcoming masterclass…

CHAPTER 7

Activate Lead Engine

Yes, I am super charged to activate the lead engine for your business. I want this for each one of you to finally convert the high-qualifying leads to prospects and finally to become your high profitable clients forever.

Thus, there are 2 concepts of getting of the entire game of marketing which are Lead Generation and Lead Nurturing. Thus, as discussed prior, the formula for Get Instant Leads is:

The reason formula is written again is that once we target your audience by making the **nano videos on any platform** that would generate the **maximum leads** for you….whether done in an organic way or the paid mode.

Moreover, once you get the **high qualified leads,** you need to activate your leads engine to allow you to reach your final destination. The final destination for you should be how to convert these leads to **Money** that will come again and again from **high profitable clients** forever. I need to tell you that Nano videos have helped me in a massive way to increase our **conversions** in Ecoste.

Why Nano Videos Work?

I have covered great insights on video marketing which proves that video is and will be the best method to convey your marketing communications/message. Allow me to share one Quote from my mentor which would sync in you in a deeper way:

> **"Don't Try to attract success, But become that attractive that success wants to attract you."**

Thus, now being honest to you, ask yourself a single question. If your prospect has an access to Nano video for his every need, desire & problem, would your business not grow?

It has the power to give an upside flip growth to your entire business. Moreover, I am reminded to highlight one fact he always repeats.

> **"People do not follow/buy products and people follow people."**

Lemme ask you a question:

"Do you want to become an **ambassador for your brand and Industry** as well?"

Thus, once your face in every nano video would be aligned on all mediums, it will make you an ambassador of your industry..My friend, taking you back to Ecoste, if you just type Ecoste you will see a similar face in 100+ videos which have been viewed on Youtube by more than 10 Million times and subscribed by close to a 100,000 Subscribers. This has empowered us to compete with a 200 Crore brand and also compete with 2000 Crore brands like Green and Century.

It has also initiated great awareness and educated the whole subject in the market. The side effect of just these 100 Nano videos is that it has made Ecoste Synonymous with Wood polymer composite product & a training school which will make the research cheaper, better and faster for the customers in Pain. Allow me to ask you some Questions:

1. Would it be an awesome deal if you get **10 to 50 leads** and activate your lead engine in a few months' time ?
2. How would it be, if your face become **ambassador for your brand & Industry?**
3. Would it not be awesome that you **activate your lead engine** which automatically gives you more leads than you can even handle?
4. Don't you want more **profitable clients** from these qualified leads which gives you growth by leaps and bounds?
5. Do you want to clone yourself by sharing knowledge which can be consumed multiple times giving you **abundance of freedom**?
6. Would it not be an amazing deal, if your lead to deal (*i.e.*) **Sales conversion cycle reduces** and your revenue increases?

7. How would that be that **you do not** have to employ a **field sales force** and can develop an **inside sales machine**?

If your answer is **YES**…..for all the above questions, then certainly, you trust in the results that I have achieved even if you're today at what so ever stage. Put a hand on your heart and say:

"If Nano videos can give him the results, I will also get it."

And Lastly say

What's the **next Action**?

I am certain that you must have got great value from teachings we have discussed from the best masters (i've learned from). This will surely help you in a great way…

More Videos every week will be uploaded on Youtube to make your marketing easy. Also, online courses (which are under production) will also be released by May 2020 for You.

The journey we spent together while reading this book, connected me to you at a deeper level…I am super excited to serve you now as my friend…Give all which will surely help you in your journey of marketing to get what you want in your Life…Now, I can feel the happiness of your success… the liveliness of your spirit floating in abundance of growth….

And, the first action…is that… I would like to invite you to my upcoming master class which is a one day workshop on How to **"Get Instant Leads"** and reserve your seat out the limited seat we may have for you Now... Log on to www.ankurhora.com

"My Purpose is to help enough people to get what they want in their life, which would give me enough to get what I want (To accomplish my mission)..."

Looking forward to **serve** You…

Name: Ankur Hora

Email: Info@ankurhora.com

Website: www.ankurhora.com

www.ingramcontent.com/pod-product-compliance
Lightning Source LLC
LaVergne TN
LVHW061042070526
838201LV00073B/5151